How to Start Day Trade

A Guide for Beginner's That Will Allow You to Have Good Profits, Through Money Management and Trading Psychology

By
Lukas Bagopym

date, and reliable, complete information. No warranties of any kind are declared or implied. Readers acknowledge that the author is not engaging in the rendering of legal, financial, medical or professional advice. The content within this book has been derived from various sources. Please consult a licensed professional before attempting any techniques outlined in this book.

By reading this document, the reader agrees that under no circumstances is the author responsible for any losses, direct or indirect, which are incurred as a result of the use of information contained within this document, including, but not limited to, — errors, omissions, or inaccuracies.

Table Of Contents

UNDERSTANDING DAY TRADING

Selecting a Platform

When settling on trading platforms, traders and financial specialists ought to consider both the expenses in question and highlights accessible. Day traders may require highlights like Level 2 statements and market producer profundity outlines to aid dynamic. In contrast, options traders may require tools that are explicitly intended to envision options systems.

Charges are another significant consideration while picking trading platforms. For instance, traders who utilize scalping as a trading strategy will float towards platforms with low expenses. By and large, lower fees are consistently ideal, yet there might be trade-offs to consider. For instance, low charges may not be favorable if they mean fewer highlights and enlightening exploration.

Some trading platforms might be rationalist to a particular middle person or broker, while other trading platforms are just accessible when working with a specific delegate or broker. Accordingly, financial specialists ought to likewise consider the notoriety of the middle person or broker before focusing on a particular trading platform to execute trades and deal with their records.

At long last, trading platforms may have explicit prerequisites to meet all requirements for their utilization. For instance, day trading platforms may necessitate that traders have, in any event, $25,000 in value in their records and be endorsed for margin trading. In contrast, options platforms may expect endorsement to trade different sorts of options before having the option to utilize the trading platform.

Mainstream Trading Platforms

There are hundreds—if not thousands—of various trading platforms, including these four great options:

• Interactive Brokers: Interactive Brokers is the most well-known trading platform for experts with low expenses and access to markets far and wide.

• TradeStation: TradeStation is a mainstream trading platform for algorithmic traders that want to execute trading techniques utilizing mechanized contents created with Easy Language.

• TDAmeritrade: TDAmeritrade is a mainstream broker for the two traders and speculators, particularly following its procurement of ThinkorSwim and the advancement of the Trade Architect platforms.

- Robinhood: Robinhood is a without commission trading platform focused at twenty to thirty-year-olds. It began as a versatile application and now has a web interface also. The platform brings in money from a few sources, from enthusiasm on money in its records to selling order stream to large brokerages.

The most well-known platform for some foreign trade (forex) market members is MetaTrader, which is a trading platform that interfaces with a wide range of brokers. Its MQL scripting language has become a famous tool for those hoping to robotize trading in monetary forms.

Picking the Right Day-Trading Software

PC applications have made it simple to mechanize trading, particularly for short-term escalated exercises like day trading, making the utilization of trading software extremely mainstream. The discussion proceeds over the profit potential that can be practically gotten from day-trading exercises utilizing web-based trading platforms, as brokerage expenses and commissions are said to remove the significant bit of accessible profit potential. It hence turns out to be critical to choose the correct day-trading software with a money-saving advantage analysis, evaluation of its pertinence to unique trading needs and systems, just as the highlights and capacities you need.

Day trading is a period bound trading action where buy or sell positions are taken and shut on a similar trading day with an expectation to make profits in littler price differentials on enormous order volumes by visit buying and selling, for the most part on leverage.

• Day trading software involve tools and order entry platforms that permit day traders to complete their work effectively and predictably.

• These platforms frequently incorporate computerized trading dependent on boundaries set trader continuously, considering orders to be sent to the market speedier than human reflexes.

• Choosing the correct day trading software framework requires understanding the expenses and advantages of each offering and if you will expand its usefulness.

What Is Day-Trading Software?

Day-trading software comprises a PC program, for the most part, given by brokerage firms, to assist customers with doing their day-trading exercises productively and conveniently. They frequently computerize analysis and enter trades on that empower traders to harvest profits that would be hard to accomplish by simple humans. For instance, a day trader may think that it's difficult to physically follow two technical indicators (like 50-and 200-day moving averages) on three individual stocks of their decision. However, a computerized day-trading software can without much of a stretch do it and spot trades once the set rules are met.

The highlights and capacities accessible may contrast starting with one software bundle then onto the next and may come in various renditions. Aside from brokers, free sellers likewise give day-trading software, which will, in general, have further developed highlights.

How Does Day-Trading Software Work?

Three fundamental highlights of any day-trading software include:

• Functionality permitting the arrangement of trading strategy (in light of technical indicators, news, trading signs or pattern acknowledgment) in the trading framework

• Automated order putting capacity (for the most part with Direct Market Access) when the measures are met

• Analytical tools to proceed with the evaluation of existing holdings (assuming any), market advancements and highlights to in like manner follow up on them

Any day-trading software will require a one-time arrangement of trading strategy along with setting the trading limits, putting the framework on live information, and letting it execute the trades.

A straightforward model: Assume stock ABC is double recorded on both the New York Stock Exchange (NYSE) and Nasdaq. You are searching for arbitrage openings, and there is a day-trading software accessible for it. You set up the accompanying:

• Select the stock ABC for arbitrage and select two markets (NYSE and Nasdaq) for trading.

• Assuming the two legs of intraday trade costs you an aggregate of $0.10 per share for brokerage and commission, you plan to search for price differentials between the two markets in the overabundance of that sum, i.e., the software ought to execute a concurrent buy and sell order just if the offer and ask prices on the two markets are varying by $0.20 (or more).

• Set the number of offers to be purchased and sold in one order (say 10,000 offers).

• Let this arrangement go live.

Further upgrades in the above software may incorporate stop-loss highlights—state if just your buy trade gets executed; however, not the sell trade. In what capacity should the day-trading software continue with the long position? Two or three options can be incorporated as upgraded highlights in the software:

• Continue to search for sell openings at recognized prices for a particular time. If no open doors are distinguished in the predefined time, make right the position at a loss.

• Set stop-loss limits and square off the buy order, if the limit is hit

• Switch to an averaging strategy—buy more stocks at lower prices to lessen the general price

Highlights and Functionality

The above is a case of arbitrage where trading openings are short-lived. A great deal of these kinds of day-trading exercises can be set up through day-trading software, and subsequently, it turns out to be critical to choose the correct one coordinating your needs. A few attributes of good day-trading software:

• Platform autonomy: Unless a trader is running profoundly complex calculations for day-trading requiring outstanding quality devoted PCs, it is fitting to go with an online software offering. Advantages incorporate availability from anyplace, no manual establishments of overhauls, and no support costs. In any case, if you are utilizing exceptionally complex calculations that require propelled registering, at that point, it is smarter to consider devoted PC based installable software, even though that will be exorbitant.

• Your exact requirements for day trading: Are you following a straightforward day-trading strategy of the moving-average following on stocks, or would you say you are hoping to actualize a mind-boggling delta-unbiased trading strategy including options and stocks? Do you need a forex feed, or would you assume you are trading on specific items like twofold options? Believing the cases on stockbrokers' site content isn't sufficient to comprehend the contribution. Order a preliminary rendition and altogether evaluate it during the underlying stage. On the other hand, check the screen-by-screen instructional exercise (if accessible) from the stockbroker or seller to plainly comprehend an ideal choice for your day-trading needs.

• Additional Features: Day trading endeavors to gain by short term price developments during the day. Such short-term price developments are thus determined essentially by the news and flexibly and order (among different components). Does your day-trading strategy require news, diagrams, Level 2 information, and select network to specific markets (like OTC), explicit information channels, and so forth? Provided that this is true, are these remembered for the software, or would the trader need to buy into them independently from different sources, consequently expanding the cost?

•   Analytical Features: Pay regard for the arrangement of explanatory highlights it offers. Here is a couple of them:

1.   Technical   Indicators/Pattern Recognition: For traders who endeavor to profit by anticipating the future price level and direction, an abundance of technical indicators is accessible. When the trader concludes the technical indicators to follow, they ought to guarantee that the day-trading software bolsters the vital robotization for effective handling of trades dependent on the ideal technical indicator.

2.   Arbitrage Opportunities Recognition: To profit by the slight price contrast of a double recorded offer on various markets, simultaneous buying (at a low price trade) and selling (at a significant expense market)

empowers profit openings and is one of the regularly followed techniques utilizing day-trading software. This requires an association with the two markets, the capacity to check price contrasts as they happen, and execute trades in an ideal way.

3. A mathematical model based systems: Few computerized trading procedures dependent on numerical models exist—like the delta-impartial trading strategy—that permit trading on a mix of options and its hidden security, where trades are set to balance positive and negative deltas with the goal that the portfolio delta is kept up at zero. The day-trading software ought to have the in-assembled insight to evaluate the current holdings, confirm accessible market prices, and execute trades for both value and options varying.

4. Trend after systems: Another enormous arrangement of methodologies generally executed through day-trading software.

Cost and Other Considerations

Anything is possible with PC programming and robotized software frameworks. Everything without exception can be robotized, with loads of customizations. Aside from choosing the correct software, it is imperative to test the recognized systems on recorded information (limiting the brokerage costs), survey the reasonable profit potential, and the effect of day-trading software costs and, at precisely that point, go for membership. This is another territory to assess; the same number of brokers do offer backtesting usefulness on their software platforms.

- Cost of software: Is the software accessible as a piece of a standard brokerage account, or does it come at an extra cost? Contingent upon your trading movement, the money-saving advantage analysis ought to be completed. Care ought to be taken to survey the accessible adaptations and their highlights. Most trading software comes free, of course, with a standard brokerage account; however, it may not have all the necessary highlights meeting your trading needs. Make certain to check the expenses of higher renditions, which might be substantially higher than the standard one. These expenses ought to be limited in assessing the profits from trading and choices made dependent on the reasonable increases.

• Price Accuracy: Does the broker and day-trading software support NBBO (national best offer and offer)? Brokers who are NBBO members are required to execute the customer trades at the best available offer and ask price, guaranteeing price intensity. Contingent on the nation's explicit guidelines, brokers may (or may not) be ordered to give the best offer and ask prices. Traders trading global protections with universal brokers and software ought to think about affirming this for the particular market.

• Protective Features: It's energizing to have software bring in money for you, however insurance is vital. With the progression of innovation, there likewise exist "sniffing calculations and software" that endeavor to distinguish the opposite side orders in the market. They are intended to permit their proprietors to profit it by "detecting" the orders on the opposite side. It will merit considering if your day-trading software is helpless against such sniffing or whether it has preventive highlights to shroud presentation to other market members.

There are unlimited skylines to investigate with trading utilizing PC programs and computerized software frameworks. It might be amazingly energizing to bring in money at the snap of a catch. Yet, one should be completely mindful of what's going in the background: Is the mechanized order is getting at the correct price in the correct market, is it following the correct strategy, etc. Many trading oddities have been credited to computerized trading frameworks. An intensive assessment of day-trading software with an away from your ideal trading strategy can permit singular traders to receive the rewards of robotized day trading.

Picking an Online Stock Broker

Profitable contributing requires you to utilize a brokerage administration that lines up with your contributing objectives, instructive needs, and learning style. Particularly for new financial specialists, choosing the best online stock broker that meets your requirements can mean the distinction between an energizing new salary stream and baffling dissatisfaction.

While there's no certain fire approach to ensure investment returns, there is an approach to set yourself up for progress by choosing the online brokerage that best suits your requirements. In this guide, we'll separate all that you should search for in your optimal brokerage, from the self-evident (like whether the platform permits you to trade the protections you're keen on) to the not self-evident (like that it is so natural to get support from a genuine human when you need it).

Notes

•   Access to the budgetary markets is cheap and straightforward gratitude to an assortment of rebate brokers that work through online platforms.

•   Different online brokers are enhanced for another sort of customer—from long-term buy-and-hold beginners to dynamic and advanced day traders.

•   Choosing the privileged online broker requires some due persistence to take full advantage of your money. Follow the means and appeal in this article to pick right.

Stage 1: Know Your Needs

Before you begin tapping on brokerage promotions, pause for a minute to focus on what's generally essential to you in a trading platform. The appropriate response will be marginally extraordinary, relying upon your investment objectives and where you are in the investment expectation to absorb information.

In case you're merely beginning, you may organize highlights like fundamental instructive assets, thorough glossaries, simple access to help staff, and the capacity to put practice trades before you begin playing with genuine money.

If you have some investment experience effectively added to your repertoire. Yet, you're hoping to quit fooling around, and you may need all the more elevated level training and assessment based assets composed by proficient speculators and investigators, just as a decent choice of crucial and technical information.

A genuinely experienced financial specialist, maybe somebody that is executed many trades as of now yet is searching for another brokerage, will organize progressed graphing capacities, contingent order options, and the capacity to trade subsidiaries, shared assets, items, and fixed-pay protections, just as stocks.

Be upfront with yourself about where you are correct now in your contributing excursion and where you need to go. Is it true that you are hoping to build up a retirement store and spotlight on aloof investments that will create tax-exempt pay in an IRA or 401(k)? Would you like to take practice at day-trading however don't have the foggiest idea where to begin? Do you like tweaking and fitting your portfolio, or would you say you will pay an expert to guarantee it's done well?

Contingent upon which way you need to follow, there might be a lot more inquiries you'll have to reply along the route as you gain understanding and refine your objectives. Until further notice, in any case, start with these four pivotal considerations to assist you with figuring out which of the brokerage highlights we talk about beneath will be generally critical to you. To help get those expository juices streaming, we've incorporated a few example inquiries under each more great point:

1. Generally, would you say you are a functioning or latent financial specialist? Would you like to be super involved and execute day-or swing-trades? Do you see yourself leaving the 9-to-5 pound and turning into a full-time financial specialist? Or, on the other hand, rather, would you like to locate a couple of strong investments to hold for the long take with next to zero day-to-day interaction?

2. How much do you definitely know? What sort of trades will you need to execute? Is it true that you will be the kind of speculator that knows what they need to do and simply needs a platform that makes it speedy and straightforward to execute trades, or do you need a broker with a more extensive range of assets to assist you with

recognizing openings? What sort of protections would you say you are centered around? Stocks, shared assets, ETFs? If you are further developed, would you additionally like to trade options, futures, and fixed-pay protections? Shouldn't something be said about margin trading? Do you need access to restrictive orders, broadened hours trading, and robotized trading options?

3. Do you need assistance? What kind? Would you like to go the DIY course, figure out how to decipher outlines and money related information to discover and execute your trades, or would you want to enlist a professional? If you need to do it without anyone's help, where are you on the expectation to absorb information? What kind of assets will you have to assist your insight? Will you need simple access to help the workforce, or would you say you are ready to realize what you have to know through instructive online assets? It is correct to say that you are glad to execute trades on the web, or will you need to bring

in to have a broker help you with the procedure?

4. What are your objectives? What are you contributing to? Is there a particular occasion or cost you need to finance? Do you expect this to, in the long run, become your essential salary source? Is it correct to say that you are attempting to develop retirement investment funds and, assuming this is the case, do you, as of now, have a retirement account, or will you need to open another one with your picked brokerage?

There are no off-base responses to these inquiries. Be upfront with yourself about how much time, vitality, and exertion you're willing and ready to place into your investments. Your answers may change after some time, and that is alright. Try not to attempt to envision every one of your needs and objectives for a fantastic remainder. Simply start with where you are at present.

Stage 2: Narrow the Field

Since you have an away from what your investment objectives are and what fundamental administrations you'll search for in your optimal brokerage, it's an ideal opportunity to trim your options apiece. While there are sure, brokerage includes that will be more significant for certain financial specialists than for other people. With such a wide range of accessible options, keeping an eye on these necessities is an incredible method to limit the field rapidly.

Stock Broker Regulation and Trust

Is the brokerage an individual from the Securities Investor Protection Corporation (SIPC)? There will commonly be documentation or disclaimer at the base of the landing page. You can rapidly look into the brokerage on the SIPC site.

Is the brokerage an individual from the Financial Industry Regulatory Authority (FINRA)? This ought to likewise be noted in a simple to-discover area. You can look into brokerages on FINRA's Broker.

If the brokerage offers checking or bank accounts, or some other store items, would they say they are secured by the Federal Deposit Insurance Corporation (FDIC)? Investment items -,, for example, brokerage or retirement accounts that put resources into stocks, bonds, options, and annuities – are not FDIC protected because the estimation of investments can't be ensured. If the brokerage offers CDs, Money Market Deposit Accounts (MMDAs), checking, or bank accounts, in any case, they ought to be entirely sponsored by the FDIC.

What sort of protection do they give to ensure you if the organization fizzles? As an individual from the SIPC, the organization ought to have protection with a for each client limit of at any rate $500,000, with $250,000 accessible for money claims. If the organization sticks to the Customer Protection Rule, it ought to likewise give extra inclusion well beyond the necessities of the SIPC.

Is there any sort of assurance of insurance against extortion? Will the organization repay you for losses coming about because of misrepresentation? Ensure you double-check what the brokerage expects of you with the goal for you to be repaid. See whether you need to give any documentation or avoid potential risks to ensure yourself.

What are current clients saying? Have a go at skimming on the web for shopper audits of the brokerage, utilizing catchphrases like "protection guarantee," "extortion insurance" and "client assistance." obviously, online surveys ought to ordinarily be thought about while considering other factors – a few people simply prefer to grumble. Notwithstanding, if there are a few clients from various destinations all housing a similar objection, then you might need to examine further.

Online Security and Account Protection

It's critical to realize how well a brokerage causes you to secure your data. Does the brokerage site offer two-factor validation? Do you have the option of actuating a security include notwithstanding your secret word? Regular options can incorporate responding to security questions, accepting exceptional, time-delicate codes through text or email, or utilizing a physical security key that openings into your USB port.

What sort of innovation does the broker use to protect your record? See whether the broker uses encryption or "treats," and if it clarifies how it utilizes them to secure your record data and how they work. Does the organization ever sell client data to outsiders, similar to publicists? The appropriate response should be no.

Brokerage Account Offerings

Since the sorts of tools you need will rely upon your objectives, you ought to likewise do a snappy check for the accompanying things to get rid of brokerages that essentially won't address your issues.

What sorts of records does the broker offer other than standard (available) investment accounts? For instance, if you have wards, see whether you can open an Education Savings Account (ESA) or a custodial record for your youngster or different wards. Would you be able to open a retirement account? Investigate whether the broker offers Roth or customary retirement accounts and if you can turn over a current 401K or IRA.

Are there various items for various contributing objectives? For instance, see whether the broker offers oversaw accounts. Additionally, see whether there investment essentials for multiple sorts of records. Would you be able to manage retirement represents representatives through the brokerage? This may apply in case you're an entrepreneur. These sorts of records incorporate SIMPLE or SEP IRAs. Does the brokerage offer Self-Directed IRAs or Solo

401K options? This applies if the main worker in your private venture is you.

Stage 3: Figure Out the Fees

While there might be different things that issue more to you than charges, you should begin with an entirely away from the amount you'll pay to utilize a specific brokerage.

For approximately, a little premium might be legitimate if the platform offers includes that its less expensive rivals need. As a rule, nonetheless, you need to lose as meager of your investment returns as conceivable to bookkeeping charges and trading commissions.

By beginning with the reality, you can without much of a stretch figure out which stockbrokers are too pricey to even think about considering and which basically aren't perfect with the sort of investment action you've centered around.

Broker Account Fees

Does the broker charge an expense for opening a record?

Is there a store, at least? Remember that common asset frequently have investment essentials of $1,000 or more. However, that is not equivalent to a brokerage necessitating that you store a base measure of money just to open a record.

Are there any yearly or month to month account upkeep expenses? Provided that this is true, would they say they are deferred for more significant records, or is there a simple method to keep away from them regardless of whether your record balance is little? For instance, Vanguard defers its yearly charge if account holders consent to get reports electronically.

Does the broker offer access to a trading platform as a feature of their free enrollment? In case you're merely beginning, the open platform may suit your necessities impeccably.

Is there a Pro or Advanced trading platform that is pay-to-play? In case you're a further developed financial specialist, it's imperative to know whether you'll have to pay to update your record to get to tools and assets that are up to your speed. Some propelled platforms are free for clients who consent to put a base number of trades every year or contribute a base sum.

What are the margin rates? Margin trading is just for experienced speculators who comprehend the risks in question. In case you're another financial specialist, this point won't concern you.

What's the base credit sum and record balance? Most brokerages will offer lower loan fees for bigger sums; however, don't leave that alone the explanation you obtain more than you should.

Is the commission plan helpful for the sort of trading you'd do? It is right to say that you are rewarded or punished for increasingly dynamic trading? For instance, Vanguard's bonus rates increments after the initial 25 trades for Standard and Flagship clients, or after the initial 100 trades for Flagship Select clients, as should be evident in the diagram above. This implies clients that emphasis on latent, buy-and-hold contributing receive the most reward.

On the other hand, E-TRADE offers decreased commissions after the initial 30 trades in some random quarters, so dynamic traders are rewarded for utilizing the platform all the more frequently. If the broker offers warning administrations, what amount do they cost? Is there a base record balance required to fit the bill for those administrations? In case you're not hoping to deal with your portfolio out of the blue, ensure you focus on consultant charges intently.

Stage 4: Test the Broker's Platform

While any brokerage ought to have a better than average depiction of what sorts of tools and assets their trading platform offers, in some cases, the ideal approach to survey platform quality is to give it a test drive. For brokers that permit you to open a record for nothing, it might even merit the push to experience the information exchange process just to get to the trading platform if that is what's fundamental.

Regardless of whether the brokerage has an electronic platform that anybody can get to or a free downloadable platform that requires no-strings information exchange, do what you can to get to the tools you'd use for nothing.
Regardless of whether you're a further developed trader, and there's no free method to mess with "Professional" tools, you can get a smart thought of the nature of a brokerage's contributions just by taking a gander at its fundamental suite. If there's

nothing in the standard platform that appears to be encouraging, it's far-fetched the propelled platform will merit your time either.

Then again, a few organizations offer a large exhibit of tools and assets with their free items, so don't discount brokerages with just a single platform right now. We've just invested a decent measure of energy, narrowing your decisions dependent on price and fundamental record contributions. Since we've at last gotten to the great stuff, ensure you invest energy taking a gander at the highlights accessible in various regions.

Make an insincere effort of putting trade to perceive how easily the procedure works. Pull up numerous statements for stocks and different protections, and snap-on each tab to understand what sort of information the platform gives. You ought to likewise look at any accessible screeners, or various tools gave to assist you with discovering investments that meet specific standards.

Inquiries to Answer While Testing Platforms

What sorts of protections would you be able to trade on the platform? You should, as of now, have precluded any platforms that don't permit you to trade the protections you're keen on. Ensure this platform consequently permit you to trade favored offers, IPOs, options, futures, or fixed-salary protections. If you don't see specific security on the platform, yet you realize that the brokerage bolsters it, have a go at glancing in your record settings, or doing a speedy hunt, to perceive how you can actuate those highlights and find out about consent necessities.

Are cites progressively? Is it correct to say that they are spilling? There will be different ways you can pull up a price quote for given security. Not every one of them will give the most exceptional information. Ensure you know about where you can discover continuous gushing data to guarantee your trades are very much coordinated. Vanguard's online platform, for instance, gives constant information in its Ticker Profile pages, yet it requires manual reviving. Basic statement level information is deferred by 20 minutes or more. Schwab's online statements likewise need manual refreshing, yet the downloadable Street-smart Edge platform and its cloud-based partner both offer continuous spilling information.

Would you be able to set up tweaked watch lists and cautions? In case you are a progressively dynamic trader, you'll likely need to have the option to get ready warnings using text, notwithstanding email, and set up various watch lists dependent on various standards.

Does the platform give screeners that you can alter to discover stocks, ETFs, common assets, or different protections that meet your particular models? Regardless of whether you're fresh out of the plastic new and have no clue about what any of the options mean, mess with the different boundaries to get a thought of how simple the tools are to utilize. A decent platform will be instinctively composed and straightforward to work.

What sorts of orders would you be able to put? Make an insincere effort to set a trade and investigate what kinds of orders are advertised. A fundamental platform should offer in any event market, limit, stop and stop limit. A superior platform will likewise permit you to put in following stop orders, or market-on-close orders (which execute at the price the security comes to at market shutting).

In case you're hoping to make moderately barely any trades, and you're not intrigued by day-or swing-trading, a fundamental choice of order types ought to be okay. If you're expecting to get into the low of stock trading, in any case, you should search for a more extensive determination. In case you're further developed, you should search for the capacity to put in contingent orders that permit you to set up numerous trades with explicit triggers that will execute consequently when your predefined conditions are met.

Stage 5: How Well Does the Stock Broker Educate Its Clients?

While a helpful and useable trading platform is significant, you ought to likewise set aside the effort to examine the brokerage's instructive contributions and evaluate the pursuit work.

In case you're another financial specialist, you should have the option to look for terms you don't have the foggiest idea or discover guidance on the most proficient method to decipher the information. If there's a subject you've been pondering about or a metric you don't comprehend, do a preliminary run utilizing the inquiry capacity and check whether you can discover the data you need rapidly and proficiently.

Keep in mind, what's intuitive and easy to understand for one financial specialist might be a terrible labyrinth of unproductive quest inquiries for another, so it's critical to discover a platform that you can work with.

When you've gone through 20 minutes or so cruising a platform, you ought to have the option to address the accompanying inquiries pretty without any problem. If you can't, and a brisk quest of the site for specific answers doesn't yield the essential data, it's feasible a sign that the brokerage's platform isn't for you.

Stock Broker's Quality and Usability

All the instructive assets on the planet are pointless if you can't get to them without any problem. A decent platform or site ought to give a wide range of instructive contributions, in different mediums, to ensure clients can rapidly and effectively discover the data they need in a configuration that works for their learning style. Before we plunge into the particular kinds of instructive assets, you ought to anticipate from a decent brokerage, and we should initially ensure those assets are easy to understand.

Utilizing Paper Trading to Practice Day Trading

Day trading has gotten fantastically serious with the flood of fast trading and algorithmic trading occurring in the markets. Fortunately, numerous online brokers have empowered paper trading records to assist traders with sharpening their aptitudes before submitting any genuine capital.

Notes

•   If you're considering turning into a day trader, it bodes well to get some sensible practice in first to try things out.

•   Paper trading is an approach to mimic trading methodologies and perceive how they would have paid off, or not, in all actuality.

•   Online brokerage platforms progressively permit new paper trading capacities through demo accounts or as an element for its current clients.

What Is Paper Trading?

Paper trading is another term for reproduced trading, whereby people can buy and sell protections without risking genuine money. While it's conceivable to backtest trading techniques, traders might be enticed to use past data to make current trades—known as the look-ahead bias—while an inappropriate backtesting dataset could include a survivorship bias. Survivorship bias is the inclination to see the exhibition of existing assets in the market as an agent test.

Speculators might have the option to mimic trading with a straightforward spreadsheet or even pen-and-paper. However, day traders would have a serious troublesome time recording hundreds or thousands of transactions for each day by hand and ascertaining their benefits and losses. Luckily, numerous online brokers and some monetary distributions offer paper trading represents people to rehearse before submitting positive cash-flow to the market.

Setting Up a Day Trading Account

Day traders ought to in a perfect world paper trade with that day trading broker they intend to use for their live record since it will be as near reality as could be expected under the circumstances.

As you search for the best spot where to rehearse your trades, consider paper trading platforms that offer live market takes care of before you start with genuine capital. This is significant because you'll need to have the option to trade without postponed feeds or handling orders.

Among the most well-known brokers are Interactive Brokers and TradeStation, which both have completely highlighted test systems that even work utilizing their mechanized trading rules. Day traders using these platforms should open a record to utilize the test system, which may mean keeping the base financing prerequisites. Fortunately, traders can utilize the test system before making live trades with their capital.

Online brokers, for example, Fidelity and TD Ameritrade likewise offer customers paper trade accounts. It's critical to remember there are still a few contrasts among reenacted and live trading. On a technical level, test systems may not represent slippage, spreads, or commissions, which can significantly affect day trading returns. On a mental level, traders may have a simpler time holding fast to trading framework rules without genuine money on the line—especially when the trading framework isn't performing admirably.

Tips for Paper Trading

Day trading relies to a great extent upon the strategy that is being utilized for trading. Some time or other traders are centered on "feel" and should depend on paper trading accounts alone, while others use computerized trading frameworks and may backtest several structures before paper trading just the most encouraging ones. Traders ought to pick the best broker platform for their requirements dependent on their trading inclinations and paper trade on those records.

At the point when paper trading, it's critical to keep a precise record of trading execution and track the strategy over a long time. A few procedures may just work in positively trending markets, which implies traders can be found napping when a bear market goes along. It's critical to test enough protections in an assortment of market conditions to guarantee their techniques hold up effectively and produce the most elevated risk-balanced returns.

At long last, paper trading is certainly not a one-time-just undertaking. Day traders ought to consistently utilize paper trading highlights on their brokerage records to test new and test techniques to attempt their hand in trading markets. Basic missteps can be inconceivably expensive for day traders who risk a considerable number of dollars in several trades every day. This makes paper trading a necessary piece of long-term achievement.

Merits of Paper Trading

Beginning with a paper trading record can help shorten your expectation to absorb information. However, there are different advantages past simply instructing yourself. To start with, you have no risk. Since you're not utilizing genuine money, you don't lose anything. You can break what mix-ups you've made and help make a winning strategy. This additionally causes you to assemble your certainty, permits you to rehearse procedures, and systems should have been a fruitful day trader, including profit or loss taking and pre-market preparation. At long last, it removes the pressure from trading. You can focus on your methodologies in a casual situation and remove the feeling from trading.

Demerits of Paper-Trading

Since it doesn't utilize genuine money, you don't get a thought of how expenses and commissions factor into your trades. These test systems additionally don't precisely mirror the truth of the markets, with the lows and highs and the feeling that accompanies trading. Hence, recollect this is a recreated domain as you get your trading abilities under tight restraints.

Practice, Practice, Practice

In case you're a first-time financial specialist, take as much time as possible paper trading before you escape and start live trading. Make sure to investigate various systems and new thoughts so you can get settled. The theory behind utilizing test systems is for you to get paid and cut down your expectation to absorb information.

When you feel like you've aced all that you can be utilizing a test system, have a go at trading with a stock that has had an anticipated run—with a lower price and a steady reaction to market conditions. If you begin trading with an exceptionally unpredictable stock, it might be a test. In any case, if you pick something more secure, you can rehearse what you've realized without taking on an excessive amount of risk.

Day traders face exceptional rivalry with regards to effectively recognizing and executing trade openings. Luckily, most online brokers offer paper trading usefulness that engages day traders to rehearse their aptitudes before submitting natural capital. Traders should exploit these highlights to forestall committing expensive errors and boost their long-term risk-balanced returns and execution.

DAY TRADING TYPES OF ORDERS

The following stage toward trading is to get comfortable with your broker's online order entry screen, and with the sorts of trading orders that might be put. Due to their significance, it merits rehashing a couple of key focuses on the three most ordinarily utilized orders.

A market order is filled at the overall price of the option or future. In light of the market's development and the potential for delay in execution, a market order might be filled at a price that varies substantially from the price showing up on your diagram or statement screen at the time you put in the order.

A limit order allows you to buy or sell at a price other than the CMP or better. It is once in a while alluded to as an "at or better" order. This is the main sort of order accessible in certain trading settings where every one of the A market order is one that will be filled at the overall price of the option or future. Due to the market's development and the potential for delay in execution, a market order might be filled at a price that contrasts essentially from the price showing up on your graph or statement screen at the time you submit the order. At the snap of a mouse, the order can be gone into the CME's steering framework for guaranteed execution or "stopped" for some time in the future.

The buy order is proposed to open a position, as opposed to finish off or spread a current short, a transaction kind of "buy open" has been determined. The trader would decide "buy close" to cover a short position, "sell open" to build up a short position, and "sell close" to finish off a long position. "Useful for the day" demonstrates the order should remain as a result until it is filled or dropped by the trader, or until the trading day closes, whichever starts things out.

One element offered by specific sites and restrictive software bundles is the "stopping" of orders. This is an amazingly important element for the dynamic day trader. Stopping alludes to determining and setting up a rundown of orders without sending them into the markets. The orders are fit to be sent on a second's notification, as quick as a key can be hit, or a mouse clicked. This spares the hour of entering all the subtleties when the second comes to put in the order. The outcome is speed and the capacity to react to an occasion rapidly and without disarray. Consider exiting a trade that is rapidly moving against you: You would prefer not to sit around idly entering the subtleties of an order. The stopped order permits you to act rapidly and conclusively to stop the loss.

Become acquainted with posting and stopping various types of orders. Most order entry screens affirm the order and require an extra action to send the order into the framework. Exploit this to work on putting in various orders because of market conduct. Post the order and, when the affirmation structure shows up, necessarily drop it. The practice is certainly required before genuine orders are set since traders need to react smoothly, absent a lot of thought when trading. After a couple of training runs, you will see that putting in an order isn't anything but difficult to achieve inside the space of a second or two. This is particularly valid for limit and stops orders, in which prices should be entered on the order entry structure.

The assignment would be simpler if traders could pull a price from one screen (e.g., examination) and duplicate it consequently into another (i.e., order entry). However, this isn't generally conceivable because of software limitations. The buy order is planned to open a position, as opposed to finish off or spread a current short, a transaction kind of "buy open" has been determined. The trader would indicate "buy close" to cover a short position, "sell open" to build up a short position, and "sell close" to finish off a long position. "Useful for the day" demonstrates the order should remain as a result until it is filled or dropped by the trader, or until the trading day closes, whichever starts things out.

One component offered by specific sites and restrictive software bundles is the "stopping" of orders. This is a precious component of the dynamic day trader. Stopping alludes to determining and setting up a rundown of orders without sending them into the markets. The orders are fit to be sent on a second's notification, as quick as a key can be hit, or a mouse clicked. This spares the hour of entering all the subtleties when the second comes to put in the order. The outcome is speed and the capacity to react to an occasion rapidly and without disarray. Consider exiting a trade that is rapidly moving against you: You would prefer not to sit around idly entering the subtleties of an order. The stopped order permits you to act quickly and conclusively to stop the loss.

Become acquainted with posting and stopping various types of orders. Most order entry screens affirm the order and require an extra action to send the order into the framework. Exploit this to work on submitting various orders in light of market conduct. Post the order and, when the affirmation structure shows up, just drop it. The practice is unquestionably required before genuine orders are set since traders need to react smoothly, absent a lot of thought when trading. After a couple of training runs, you will see that putting in an order isn't anything but difficult to achieve inside the space of a second or two.

This is particularly valid for limit and stops orders, in which prices should be entered on the order entry structure. The errand would be simpler if traders could pull a price from one screen (e.g., examination) and duplicate it consequently into another (i.e., order entry), yet this isn't generally conceivable due to software limitations. They are executed. However, not all orders might be dropped. Orders that have just been executed fall into that classification. This takes us back to the issue of deferred affirmations: A trader may wish to decline any order. However, it can't sense it has now been executed. The person simply doesn't have any acquaintance with it since affirmation has not yet been gotten. In short, retractions may fall flat as a result of timing.

Notwithstanding manual abrogation, an order might be dropped consequently. Much of the time, when a limit or stop is posted, the order stays as a result just until the finish of the trading day. When the order has not been implemented by, at that point, and has not been dropped by the trader, it kicks the bucket. Contingent upon the trading platform and trade, it might be conceivable to determine an order as "great till dropped" (GTC). This sort of order stays basically until it is either filled or effectively dropped by the trader. In certain unique situations, orders might be left as a result of just as long as 15 minutes. At any rate before the finish of the trading day, ensure that you know the status of your orders and that those you need to be dropped are gone. The day trader, for the most part, needs to end the day level (no positions held, either long or short) and without any orders pending.

How Orders Are Processed and Filled

In electronic order coordinating frameworks, orders go into the structure in lines, where they are arranged by price and time got. A PC pulls the orders (as offers and offers) out of the lines. At each price level, endeavors are made to coordinate the most established orders first. As matches happen, orders are expelled from the line. At the point when all orders on a given price level are coordinated, the related line vanishes. Coordinating at that point starts to occur at the following price level.

The way toward looking over the offers and offers to create matches is essentially prompt. Notwithstanding, when your offer or offer has arrived at the head of the queue ready to be matched, there may no longer be an offered or offer on the contrary side. This is a typical issue in illiquid markets. In such markets, specific sorts of orders (e.g., market orders) might be expensive essentially because they might be coordinated at horrible prices. In contrast, different sorts of orders (e.g., limit orders) may not be filled regardless of whether prices contact levels where a fill would be normal.

As portrayed somewhere else, different frameworks, for example, pro frameworks (e.g., NYSE, AMEX) and those of options clearinghouses, albeit comparative on a fundamental level, vary enormously in the subtleties.

Staying away from Surprises

The divergence between the price on the screen when a market order is posted and the price at which the order is occupied, the time it takes to get an affirmation, and the infrequent issue while dropping an order all add to the vulnerability engaged with trading. Consider price shocks. When attempting to build up a position in an option, future, or value, you can submit a limit order to stay away from the obnoxiousness of acquiring a fill at a more awful price than that normal. In any case, a limit order involves the risk of not getting filled by any stretch of the imagination. The chance of not getting filled (which exists with a limit) can be hazardous in this circumstance. Utilizing a market or stop order, in any case, may bring about slippage, with the exit happening at a more unfriendly price than wanted. In the following part, we will additionally talk about the management and control of risks having to do with execution and order stream, just as those related to the trading instrument or market.

Reacting to Events

The round of trading, in any event on a solid, mechanical level, is fundamentally one of investigating the market and reacting rapidly and astutely to watched occasions. Graphs and the different statements are contemplated, with no guarantees, maybe, the news.

Screech boxes are tuned in to. This is a piece of the quest for trading openings motioned by news reports, changes in the sound from the pits, or differing patterns of market conduct. These are the occasions to which a trader reacts. The key to active trading is figuring out how to perceive significant occasions and to make fitting reactions to them rapidly. Like a rodent in a Skinner box, the trader must figure out how to respond accurately to pertinent occasions and how to overlook superfluous ones.

At the point when the Day Ends

Many day traders close out most positions when the trading day closes. To forestall expensive oversights, the status of all trades ought to be checked to guarantee that no positions remain and that pending orders have been dropped. This guarantees there is no introduction to proceeding with risk. Profits and losses would then be able to be counted, and preparations made for the following trading day. As opposed to longer-term trading, day traders get quick criticism and, in this way, adapt rapidly. Rather than being assessed on a quarterly or yearly premise, execution is inspected toward the finish of every day.

What Have We Learned?

The initial step is to introduce and arrange your outlining and diagnostic software.

Teach the software to show outlines for the markets you're following.

Modify the settings for indicators, the number and sorts of bars, and the hues you like with the goal that you can get all the data you need from the diagram initially.

Set "cautions" so the program will promptly show changes in market conditions, and perhaps to flag entry and exit focuses.

At the point when first beginning, watch the markets (to build up a comprehension of their conduct, to perceive graph patterns, and so on.) and execute paper trades. Acquaint yourself with your brokerage's site and trading screens. Design them to suit your requirements.

Verify that you comprehend and realize how to utilize market, limit, and stop orders.

Figure out how to "park orders" utilizing your brokerage's trading platform. Such orders are indicated and set up on a stopped orders screen. The orders are not positioned in the market, yet are fit to be set on a second's notification.

Addition familiarity with posting orders by entering them on the trading screen and dropping them before execution.

At the point when you place orders, perceive how quickly they are affirmed. Affirmation is important, so you comprehend what further action to take in a trade. For instance, if your order doesn't get filled, you have no position to exit.

Ensure you realize how to drop orders you place.

Discover your brokerage's default order scratch-off approaches. Would you be able to indicate "great till dropped" (GTC) orders?

Are open orders consequently dropped toward the finish of a fixed timeframe except if, in any case, determined?

Electronic order coordinating frameworks place orders in lines at the diverse price levels. Inside each line, more seasoned orders get coordinated (filled) first.

Limit orders can be utilized to evade shocks, so you don't get filled at a price significantly more awful than the one you need. The trade-off is that you probably won't get a fill.

Before shutting for the afternoon, make a point to finish off the entirety of your positions (except if, obviously, you deliberately need to convey them over until the following day).

Essentials of Day Trading and Orders

The motor of profit is nothing but volatility. The more noteworthy the swings in price and the shorter the time wherein they happen, the more prominent the open door for profit. As it were, the more unique the volatility, the more prominent the profit potential. For the day trader, mainly, generally elevated levels of volatility are basic. There must be sufficient development in a short timeframe, or the day trader can't bring in money. The thought is to go all through the market rapidly, catching little profits more than once for the day. Markets that have vast and various intraday swings (e.g., the S&P 500) make high day trading vehicles.

Money Management

With volatility comes risk. Not exclusively can agile development bring a profit; if the trader is positioned effectively, it can likewise bargain a loss?

One explanation numerous individuals are pulled in to day trading is that the short time gives a deception of more noteworthy control. Since the trader works in a short time and can react rapidly to occasions, it is regularly conceivable to abridge the losses from trades that have turned out badly. If a trade moves in a negative direction, a tick of the mouse can send an exit order into the market to end the trade before much harm is finished. The trader is then all set on to the following trade. The reality in the possibility of more noteworthy control is that a gifted trader can adequately control losses a significant part of the time.

More truth dwells in the way that the day trader evades the risk of huge short-term holes and, for the most part, endeavors to manage a bigger number of little trades. The feeling of control becomes deceptive when the trader can't exit a terrible trade as fast as wanted. Market or stop order might be filled at a price that is very not the same as the one anticipated. This can undoubtedly occur during quick market conditions when the market can move fundamentally before the order is executed. Under such conditions, countless different traders may have just sent their orders into the line, so your order might be holding up in line, unexecuted, as your record lessens.

The genuine risk in day trading is the point at which the trader follows up on the dream of absolute control and trades an unreasonably enormous number of agreements or offers. If a day trader were to trade a similar number of proposals or agreements as a longer period trader, introduction to risk would be altogether less. The shorter introduction time frame in day trading implies less open door for the market to move enormous sums, and the fast reaction times offer a more noteworthy, yet not complete, level of control. Because of the more prominent control, the accomplished day trader can, without a doubt, trade more agreements or offers on an intraday premise yet needs to make a sensible evaluation of the imaginable degree of risk as per the volatility of the market being traded.

If trading 500 offers on a 2-to 3-week time period give a proper degree of risk, it may be protected to trade somewhere in the range of 1000, and 5000 offers intraday yet in all likelihood undependable to trade 50,000 offers. We are not thinking about the impacts of continuous trading as far as commissions. It is all the more expensive to day trade because the huge number of trades taken for the day prompts in total more noteworthy transaction costs (slippage and commissions). The sharp trader can limit these expenses by choosing a decent profound mark broker or specialist trading organization, and by not surrendering the spread that is, by utilizing effectively submitted limit orders as opposed to market orders.

Even though the risk of an abrupt crash is radically less for the sensibly educated and mindful day trader, the probability of making a profit is additionally not precisely for the longer-term trader. In the stock market, the consistent upward bias as of late makes it simple to succeed. In any case, in day trading, the prevailing market trend gives intraday development that is commonly inadequate to conquer transaction costs. There are, nonetheless, procedures that can help the day trader be reliably profitable. Because of the serial input and reinforcement they get, day traders have a lot more noteworthy opportunity to gain from their slip-ups. The short period likewise gives the chance to misuse the little, rehashed wasteful aspects that are found in many markets.

What are the fundamental approaches to control risk? The fundamental one has the order to execute trades that move against you unhesitatingly. Numerous individuals tend to hold on to a losing trade in the typically mixed up conviction that prices will switch, and the trade will turn profitable. Holding on to a losing position is perhaps the gravest slip-up a trader can make. Consider it. Would it be worthwhile for you to hold up more than that? Or, on the other hand, would it be a good idea for you to hold up until you get a margin call, or until the trade has disposed of your whole record? Pretty much every effective trader realizes that readiness to exit a losing trade unflinchingly is the most fundamental piece of trading. If you, despite everything, accept that the market will pivot, you can generally get back in later, most likely at an excellent price, since the market is practically sure to give various chances to reentry. Try not to stress over the additional transaction costs. They will add up to far, not exactly losing everything.

Having cut your losses rapidly, you will be around to attempt once more. If you have any edge whatsoever, odds are the following trade will be a champ. On average, there ought to be sufficient winning trades to compensate for the losing ones if the last are not allowed to become unchecked.

A choice about when a trade has turned out poorly can be founded on various standards.

Maybe some trendlines on the outline recommend that, if prices move past a specific level, the future or option is carrying on uniquely in contrast to foreseen, inciting a brisk exit. Another guideline used to decide when to exit a trade depends on volatility. The development of the market at a given time may be thought of as being made out of a trend segment and commotion: If the future or option moves against the trade more than anticipated measurably, the trade ought to be finished off. The protection of time is likewise especially important. Day traders, for the most part, manage short times. Any foreseen conduct ought to proliferate. If trade mopes, get out and proceed onward. Why be presented to expected risk, also pass up on chances that may exist somewhere else, by remaining in a trade that isn't creating profit?

These things have to do with overseeing risk, safeguarding capital, and making due to take the following trade. Keep in mind the curveballs the market can toss. Things can happen rapidly. In the next section, on trading strategies, we will examine extra techniques by which risks related to various types of trades can be controlled.

Catching Profit

Accepting you get by to take the following trade, which is the thing that overseeing risk is about, your next objective is to catch a few profits. Extraordinary traders have a platitude: "Cut losses off, yet let profits run." Almost everybody concurs with the idea of endeavoring to ride a decent wave until it begins to fail. The day trader should be somewhat more dynamic and forceful, yet it is an exercise in careful control. Get out too early, and potentially miss huge profits. Get out past the point of no return and be presented to unnecessary risk or see profits go to losses. The key thought is to sell when others are as yet buying and to buy when others are as yet selling. For instance, you buy IBM calls with a strike price of 95 for $5. After five minutes, the calls hit $6 on high volume. Buyers are especially in proof. Except if there is a convincing explanation not to, this is an ideal opportunity to sell. Why? Since now is the point at which you will get the best price.

There is extraordinary interest. The seller is the provider. What is being sold is immediately snatched by others. When the market starts to falter, getting a decent fill turns out to be increasingly troublesome and questionable. The long-term trader can bear to hold up until momentum eases back because a point or two of slippage won't have a lot of effects when managing enormous, long-term moves. However, since day traders catch little, quick moves, an additional half, quarter, or even eighth of a point has a major effect. Selling into order or buying into flexibly can give that extra eighth, quarter, or even a large portion of a point. Accordingly, when day trading, exit while momentum stays before the market eases back.

At the point when you are utilizing limit orders, buying into gracefully or selling into order brings about a more noteworthy probability of getting filled. One sophisticated approach to exit a trade, mainly if there is some projection of future price, is to submit a limit order at the anticipated price and let it sit. This ensures an exit at that price or better. Traders are utilizing Fibonacci ratios, just as help and opposition, can, in some cases, exit absolutely at the top or base of a move utilizing this method. Once more, getting a reasonable price is a significant part of being a fruitful day trader because the moves are genuinely little. Another approach to make a profit from a trade includes over and over putting in and dropping limit orders: Place an order, drop it, place another, and drop that one. Rehash the procedure until an order gets filled. If momentum starts to evaporate or there is any sign of an inversion, stop this game and put in a market order for a quick exit.

Moving limit arranges around doesn't cost anything as far as transaction charges, except if the order executes. In the realm of electronic trading, posting and dropping orders implies pushing around electrons, bits, and bytes.

Just when an order is filled, and a transaction happens, are costs brought about. Trading along these lines non-electronically (i.e., via telephone) will disturb your broker since you are giving that person a great deal of work with no reward. After a timeframe, the broker may even decline to acknowledge particular sorts of orders from you. We encountered such a difficult when trading the S&P 500 with a short-term, numerically-based trading model. Inside seven days, the brokers revolted and would not acknowledge anything other than market orders! At the point when we went along and just submitted market orders (even though they made the framework less profitable on account of the expanded slippage), the brokers got messy and may have deliberately deferred trades. With electronic trading, this issue doesn't exist. PCs couldn't care less what number of orders they endeavor to course or match. The PC won't grumble, regardless of whether a few orders are put at regular intervals. This gives an incredible edge and is perhaps the best explanation behind moving to electronic, web-based trading. It permits the trader to work in an increasingly advanced and smart way without such hindrances as miserable brokers.

All in all, put in the same number of orders and take whatever actions essential to augment your edge. Never let a profit become a loss. Never let a little loss develop into a huge one. In any event, when a future or option shows almost no movement, limit orders can be utilized to make little profits by endeavoring to buy close to the low finish of the spread and sell close to the high finish of the spread. Just a sixteenth or an eighth of a point for each trade might be caught, yet in total such trades can be very rewarding.

Utilizing Different Order Types

Numerous sorts of orders can be utilized in trading. The most widely recognized is the limit order, the market order, and (for specific markets and in specific settings) the stop order. Proficient day traders generally work with market and limit orders.

Limit orders interpret legitimately to offers or offers. At the point when you state you need to buy 100 portions of IBM at $96 limit, it implies that you need to buy those offers at the price of $96 or better. You are putting an offer for IBM shares at $96. So also, if you need to sell 100 offers at $96, you are setting an offer. It could be said, along these lines, the limit order is the local or essential order type. The principle property of a limit order is that it might be filled if it tends to be coordinated with another order at the fitting price. Coming back to the IBM model, if you place a buy at $96 limit, that is, offer $96 for 100 portions of IBM stock you may be filled if another trader has posted a proposal at $96 or better for at least 100 offers. Note that, with a limit order, there is a risk that you may just get an incomplete fill, so you probably won't get all the agreements or offers you need.

Limit orders don't ensure quick fills. For instance, if IBM is as of now offered at $96, yet it is offered at $95, and you put in a limit order to buy at $95.25 or better (inside the spread), at that point there is no other offer that can be coordinated to your offer. Somebody, notwithstanding, might see the offer and be happy to sell you the stock at your price. In dynamic markets, the offers and offers continue moving. It isn't far-fetched that, inside a couple of moments or less, your order will be filled, mainly if it is for a few offers or agreements. By utilizing the limit order, you will have acquired a price essentially superior to the current offer. Thus, the limit order is commonly a decent order for day trading. As referenced before, an additional quarter, eighth, or even sixteenth of a point can assist you with accomplishing profitability. The mechanics of submitting a limit order are canvassed in the past part, where illustrations are given.

When all is said in done, at some random time, there is a more significant expense at which offers or agreements are offered, and a lower price at which they are offered. At the point when a market order is submitted, the order is filled at the best current offer (if buying) or offer (if selling). Essentially, you are purchasing the ticket price as opposed to arranging. In the trading speech, this is "surrendering the spread." Unless there is support, for example, expecting to exit in a rush or to hop into a creating trend, day traders ought to disregard market orders.

In the above conversation, we talked as though market orders are filled momentarily and totally at the current offer or offer. In any case, the number of agreements or offers as of now being offered or offered might be a few orders in front of yours that are holding on to be executed. Your fill may, in this manner, be more terrible than anticipated. Offers and offers move around always and now and then quickly. As orders get coordinated, particular offers and offers vanish, while new ones come into the market, maybe at different prices. However, more often than not, market orders are executed inside a couple of moments.

Stop orders require the particular of a price. Stop orders are customary in the futures pits, yet are not a natural element of many direct access trading scenes, similar to the SOES, the different ECNs, or GLOBEX. These scenes don't in themselves acknowledge such orders. If your broker has a screen that permits stops to be entered for these scenes, the stop order is presumably steered to the broker, who, at that point, watches the market for your sake and, ideally, rapidly submits a market order when prices infiltrate the stop. There is no explanation you can't do this without anyone else's help. Since, as a day trader, you are effectively watching the markets, place a psychological stop or set it as an alarm in your diagramming program, and enter a market order at the proper second.

Even though stops, by and large, are not utilized by day traders in values or value options, they are being used now and again with items. However, there should be attentive, mainly when the stops are near the market. At the point when stops are set in the market, others (i.e., floor traders) become mindful of their essence and may attempt to "firearm" them. Traders on the floor may try to coordinate your order even though it is outside the current market. This can cause you a loss and give the trader on the contrary side of the trade with addition when the market comes back to the typical price.

With E-DAT, it is most likely best to just post-market orders yourself when the market infiltrates an ideal stop. To be ensured, if there should arise an occurrence of a crisis, a stop-loss order can be put far away from the market, well far from gunning. This "wide" or out of sight will just fill in as protection, while mental stops give essential risk control and money management. Utilizing this methodology, if something happens that you can't respond to (e.g., if your web association goes dor your PC crashes), you are, in any event, reasonably secured. Simultaneously, you have not parted with your hand, since the genuine stops that structure some portion of your trading plan can't be seen by others.

Stop orders are generally utilized for two purposes:

- To enter a trade in the path of momentum; and
- Control losses or lock-in paper profits.

In the two cases, don't feel depressed about changing the stops because of market action. For example, to secure an expanding paper profit, trail the market with your stop. This may require moving your stop a few times. As a feature of good trading practice, start moving the stops as you see fit, without stressing over the aggravations experienced by brokers or floor traders. Keep in mind, you are in the matter of making a profit out of this game, not making it simple for others at your cost.

Detecting the Ebb and Flow of the Market

To get a feeling of the back and forth movement of the market, start by calling up a diagram of the S&P 500, E-Mini, or maybe an at the money option on your preferred web or oil stock. Set these graphs to show movement either on a tick-by-tick or 1-minute time. If you have done different sorts of trading and know about specific indicators, put these up on the diagrams too. Indicators that are utilized by end-of-day traders, for example, moving averages, the MACD (moving average combination divergence), and stochastic, are likewise helpful to day traders. On another screen, you might need to have live market numbers: Level II NASDAQ cites, the most definite statements accessible for the underlying security, or the comparable sorts of market quotes for futures, for example, the S&P 500 or E-Mini. At that point, sit and watch the markets to figure out the kind of development to anticipate.

As you analyze different protections, you ought to have the option to build up an inclination for the sort of character the specific market is displaying at some random point in time. The thought is to watch the market in a functioning, included design for a long sufficient opportunity to build up a feeling of its present mode or character and to have the option to envision what it will do straightaway. Is it in wave mode and arriving at a base on its way to the next peak? Is it trending consistently? Is it carrying on randomly? Or, on the other hand, is it pushing in steps, shaping a sort of flight of stairs? Little top stocks, important to traders of value options, much of the time show a flight of stairs pattern in which calm levels are punctuated by prices that flood on expanded volume.

As you continued looking for more profound comprehension, have a go at changing the times on your diagrams, or calling up other outlines with longer times, to get an alternate point of view on similar markets. As you watch the markets, attempt to decide whether there are any intermittent patterns of conduct. Do certain configurations continue showing up? Maybe the volume of yelling increments at significant market tums or toward the beginning of trends. Possibly tranquil periods are set apart by moves like those in Figure 5-1. Just by watching the outlines while you tune in to the pit, will you get familiar with the trading hugeness of the different sounds?

Notwithstanding taking a gander at graphs and tuning in to a screech box, you might need to look at market action on a constant statement screen, even though not ordinarily advantageous when trading futures, the statements are helpful when trading stocks or stock options. Give specific consideration to the ask and offer prices, and, if accessible, their sizes. Likewise, think about the last, not many transactions, and, if conceivable, the number of offers or agreements included. If the data on who has posted the offeror offered isn't accessible, attempt to make a derivation.

Was it an expert, a market producer, or some other trader? Does the price of the last transaction continue flipping to and fro between the ask and the offer? This proposes a market creator buying from and selling to the general population. Every single such datum gives an understanding into current market movement, including backing and opposition levels, and where the greatest day traders (e.g., the authorities) figure they can bring in money as go-betweens by buying on the offer and selling on the ask (a strategy you can likewise utilize in specific markets).

When you know about how to call up and redo outlines and statement screens, just as how they show up and update continuously, start paper trading. You should figure out how to react to the markets, not just watch them, however, to detect their recurring pattern. To start this procedure, take a piece of paper and envision that you are going to trade the market you are viewing. As the outline scrolls, you see a point where the market is by all accounts arriving at the base of a wave. Based on the market's earlier conduct, you have a feeling that it is starting to turn around its descending excursion and is prepared to rise.

Spot a buy, along with the price and time, on the paper. Continue viewing. Is it correct to say that you are getting anxious? Maybe the market has proceeded with its plunge, causing a paper loss. Is it an opportunity to get out to stop the damage, or would it be a good idea for you to hold on? Possibly you ought to get out now before the loss develops, provided that this is true. Perhaps the market started to move for your trade not long after you said it down. You choose to hold on. As the market moves more in support of yourself, you become progressively apprehensive. You might want to sell to make your profit. Would it be advisable for you too? You falter in your choice and can't arrive at a resolution.

Possibly you should hold on and catch a conceivably colossal move. On the other hand, perhaps, the market will switch, causing your paper profit to transform into a loss. Disarray. Loss of motion. You currently observe the light the requirement for an idea out trading plan. Goodness, no. The market gives off the impression of being switching. You at long last choose to sell. Note the sell (exit), just as the time and price. You are currently out of the market. Your position is "level." You have made a paper trade.

Continue looking for another entry opportunity. At that point, do it once more. Maybe this time, you go short, anticipating that the market should drop. You experience a similar method of pausing and responding, just now it is with the expectation of buying to counterbalance your short position, as such, to exit.

After paper trading, a few times, audit your trades and perceive how well you have done. Try not to be amazed if you have lost money. To make the circumstance increasingly sensible, come back to the occasions when you exited or entered your trades and alter the prices you noted to reflect not the price present at the hour of the trade, however the most noticeably terrible price that happened inside brief after the trade choice, except that the market has given you slippage.

Keep in mind, in this analysis, and you weren't utilizing limit orders, simply market orders, so that slippage would be reasonable in genuine trading. At the point when you recalculate your trades, you will find that the losses have developed. For a much more prominent feeling of frenzy and frustration, take away commissions. Try not to be excessively disturbed. As you practice, your trading will improve.

Perhaps this isn't the situation you encountered. Maybe your trades were astoundingly profitable. Bravo. However, don't release it to your head. Your favorable luck might be because of apprentice's karma, and the real primary trade you spot might be a washout.

On the other hand, it may not. You may have a genuine feeling of the market. All things being equal, be mindful. You, despite everything, have a long way to go. A standard structure for paper trading shows up in the past section.

Work on Trading

After paper trading for some time, attempt assistance, for example, the one gave by Auditrack, or trade with genuine money, yet in little parcels. If, for instance, you have a $50,000 record and hope to trade 10 or 20 options contracts one after another, or a few thousand portions of stock, start work on trading with just one agreement or 100 shares of stock. Trade sufficiently little so that, even should you lose and commit numerous errors, you won't get injured.

The thought is to pick up involvement with something as near genuine, live trading as conceivable without acquiring the risks. If you have to participate in little scope live trading for this procedure, your losses will be, to some degree, more noteworthy than they may find some way or another be. For instance, when you trade from a minor perspective, commissions can be a significant issue. In any case, at this stage, don't concern yourself about such expenses. The thought is to get live, hands-on training with insignificant risk. If you take little losses from commissions, think of it as a preparation cost, such as taking a course. You can limit these expenses by utilizing a profound mark brokerage, something you ought to do at any rate. When you have taken in the ropes and can trade reliably, you can continuously expand the trade size.

Work on trading is totally basic to building up the capacity to trade profitably. From the outset, you may think that it's hard to react to the market with speed and precision. You might be awkward in posting and checking orders, taking significantly additional time than ideal. Try not to surge. It is smarter to be, to some degree, late than to post an order that is genuinely off-base. With training, you will pick up beauty and speed. After enough recreated or small, genuine trades, the specialists will turn out to be natural, and your feeling of the markets will additionally create.

For items day traders, Auditrack is perhaps the best help accessible for work on trading. A few brokers (e.g., Lind-Waldock) offer access to Auditrack utilizing screens as website pages, like those used for actual trades.

At the hour of this composition, Lind-Waldock offers a free, 1-month preliminary of its P.R.O.F.I.T. framework, which gives access to Auditrack. After that period, the membership charge is around $40 every month, regardless of whether you have a record with Lind-Waldock. Auditrack gives a chance to work on trading in a domain near the one you will utilize when trading. It is a finished, nitty-gritty reproduction of the whole trading process. Auditrack even keeps an individual record of each trade. At the point when paper trading, you need to keep a put the account yourself, which could take away from your planning. Auditrack, nonetheless, keeps up a recreated account and, over the net, sends its customers proclamations that even incorporate conclusions for slippage and commissions. It gives a total and sensible recreation of the whole procedure, including the subtleties. You feel like you are trading and experience feel as though money was on the line.

Utilization of such a help additionally permits you to assess your advancement as a trader handily. Auditrack is presently accessible for futures and futures options, yet not for stock options.

There are different approaches to pick up involvement with work on trading. One path is through investment in a web-based trading game or rivalry. We often depend on a recreation we created (through Scientific Consultant Services) and use it as an encouraging tool at the New York Institute of Finance: "The Trading Game." Unlike a significant number of the trading test systems referenced over, this game fills the screen with price outlines, not merely numbers. The outlines incorporate moving averages, stochastic, and an assortment of indicators. It likewise combines options reenactments, utilizing manufactured option prices created with the Black-Scholes model, from the prices on the basic stocks or futures. The game permits you to enter a trade (utilizing grouped sorts of orders) and follow its encouraging tick by tick on the outline until you choose to exit.

It monitors the number of trades put, profit per trade, average profit, and different measurements that educate you regarding your presentation. You needn't bother with a live information feed to play this game. However, you do require verifiable information. It tends to be played on any market, and on whenever outline intraday, end-of-day, whatever your inclination. The game makes a brilliant preparation tool, particularly for those keen on considering graphs and utilizing pattern acknowledgment (it even incorporates a few channels to assist). Framework traders additionally think that it's entirely significant.

To be maximally successful, work on trading must incite encounters of dread and eagerness, disarray, and loss of motion.

Except if you are a characteristic, you will find the requirement for a trading plan, a framework, and different guides to control you in your trading choices and to enable you to realize what to do in any circumstance. The thought is to build up a decent, natural feel for the market, just as the capacity to act conclusively and equitably based on your perceptions without the harming effect of feelings. This sort of aptitude and capacity can be picked up by broad work on trading, just as by having or building up a decent trading arrangement or strategy.

What Have We Learned?

Generally, elevated levels of market volatility are fundamental to day trading.

Markets can move significantly, in a short time, when volatility is high. Consequently, it is essential to limit the possible risk of the market hurrying against you.

When choosing about the number of agreements to trade, consider the risk potential should extraordinary antagonistic development happen.

Quickly exit trades that start to move against you. You can generally reappear later. The additional transaction costs are superior to the further loss of capital from holding tight to an awful trade.

Trendlines can help decide if market conduct has changed in an unforeseen manner.

Normal market conduct ought to proliferate. If a trade grieves, exit, the market has likely changed. Why open yourself to unnecessary risk?

Even though you would prefer not to stop a decent trade, it is ideal to sell while others are as yet buying into the trend. You will get a brisk deal and a generous fill. Slippage may work in support of yourself.

One great approach to exit is to continue putting in limit orders at or directly above satisfactory profit targets. You can generally drop them and spot higher ones if you feel the trend is sufficient.

Limit orders are offers to buy or offers to sell at explicit prices. Such an order may be filled if a trader on the opposite side of your position coordinates your price.

There is no assurance of a moment (or any) dispatch with a limit order. However, in dynamic markets, the probability of fill is more prominent.

Market orders are set without a special price. You are putting to buy or sell at the current market price, which (when the order gets filled) might be very not quite the same as what you expected (contingent upon the volatility of the market). They are usually filled in minutes.

Except if you have to bounce into a quick creating trend or to exit an awful trade rapidly, market orders ought to be stayed away from, particularly by day traders.

Stop arranges additionally require the determination of a price. You sell short (exit long) if prices dip under the stop order, and buy (exit short) if prices ascend above it.

Stops are utilized when trading futures or items, yet not values or value options. The

SOES, some ECNs, and GLOBEX don't acknowledge them.

If you are going to utilize stops, don't enter them as orders. Permanently remember the figure as a threshold for action to buy or sell when prices close to it.

It is most astute at putting in a stop order with your brokerage just for disaster protection purposes, so your position will be promptly finished off if something occurs (e.g., your PC accidents), and you can't react rapidly enough to market conduct. Generally, such stops are set moderately out of sight past where you would truly need to exit.

Try not to spare a moment to alter stops oftentimes as market conditions change.

Before trading with money, watch the markets important to figure out them and the sorts of practices they regularly display.

After you have a feeling of the markets from contemplating them, attempt paper trading, at that point mimicked trading or potentially trading games and rivalries. This won't just help you with understanding the markets and how to put in trading orders precisely; however, it will likewise give you knowledge into your trading style and conduct.

RISK & MONEY MANAGEMENT
Day Trading on Margin

Day trading includes buying and selling similar stocks on numerous occasions during trading hours in anticipation of securing snappy profits from the development at stock prices. Day trading is risky, as it's reliant on the variances in stock prices on one given day, and it can bring about considerable losses in a short timeframe.

• Trading on margin permits you to acquire assets from your broker to buy a bigger number of offers than the money in your record would take into account all alone. Margin trading likewise carries into account short-selling.

• By utilizing leverage, margin lets you intensify your possible returns - just as your losses.

• Margin calls and support margin are required, which can include losses in the occasion a trades turn sour.

Margin and Day Trading

Buying on margin, then again, is a tool that encourages trading in any event, for the individuals who don't have the important measure of money available. Buying on margin improves a trader's buying power by permitting them to buy for a more prominent sum than they have money for; the shortfall is filled by a brokerage firm at a premium. At the point when the two tools are consolidated as day trading on margin, risks are highlighted. Furthermore, passing by the announcement, "the higher the risk, the higher the possible return," the profits can be manifold. However, be cautioned: There are no certifications.

The Financial Industry Regulatory Authority (FINRA) rules characterize a day trade as "The buying and selling or the selling and buying of similar security around the same time in a margin account." The short-selling and buys to cover related security around the same time, along with options likewise fall under the domain of a day trade.

At the point when we talk about day trading, some may enjoy it just at times and would have distinctive margin prerequisites from the individuals who can be labeled as "pattern day traders." Let's comprehend these terms along with the margin rules and necessities by FINRA.

A term pattern day trader is utilized for somebody who executes at least four-day trades inside five business days, gave one of two things: 1) The quantity of day trades is over 6% of his complete trades in the margin account during a similar five-day duration, or 2) The individual enjoys two neglected day trade calls inside a period span of 90 days. A non-pattern day trader's record brings about day trading just once in a while.

In any case, if any of the above measures are met, at that point, a non-pattern day trader record will be assigned as a pattern day trader account. In any case, if a pattern day trader's record has not made any day trades for 60 consecutive days, at that point, its status is turned around to a non-pattern day trader account.

Margin Requirements

To trade on margin, financial specialists must store enough money or qualified protections that meet the underlying margin prerequisite with a brokerage firm. As per the Fed's Regulation T, financial specialists can get up to half of the total expense of procurement on margin, and the staying half is saved by the trader as the underlying margin necessity.

The support margin prerequisites for a pattern day trader are a lot higher than that for a non-pattern day trader. The base value necessary for a pattern day trader is $25,000 (or 25% of the all-out market estimation of protections, whichever is higher) while that for a non-pattern day trader is $2,000. Consistently trading account must meet this necessity freely and not through cross-ensuring various records. In circumstances when the record falls beneath this specified figure of $25,000, further trading isn't allowed until the record is recharged.

Margin Calls

A margin call happens if your record falls underneath the upkeep margin sum. A margin call is an interest from your brokerage for you to add money to your record or closeout positions to take your record back to the necessary level. If you don't meet the margin call, your brokerage firm can finish off any open positions to bring the record back up to the base worth. Your brokerage firm can do this even without your endorsement and can pick which position(s) to exchange. Furthermore, your brokerage firm can charge you a commission for the transaction(s). You are answerable for any losses supported during this procedure, and your brokerage firm may exchange enough offers or agreements to surpass the underlying margin necessity.

Margin Buying Power

The buying power for a day trader is multiple times the abundance of the upkeep margin as of the end of business of the earlier day (state a record has $35,000 after, the more initial day's trade, at that point the overabundance here is $10,000 as this sum is far beyond the base prerequisite of

$25,000. This would give a buying intensity of $40,000 (4 x $10,000). If this is surpassed, at that point, the trader will get a day trading margin call gave by the brokerage firm. There is a period span of five business days to meet the margin call.

Case of Trading on Margin

Expect that a trader has $20,000 more than the support margin sum. This will furnish the trader with a day trading buying intensity of $80,000 (4 x $20,000). If the trader enjoys buying $80,000 of PQR Corp at 9:40 a.m., trailed by $60,000 of XYZ Corp. at 10.00 a.m. around the same time, at that point he has surpassed his buying power limit. Regardless of whether he along these lines sells both during the evening trade, he will get a day trading margin call the following day. However, the trader could have evaded the margin cancel by selling PQR Corp before buying XYZ Corp.

Note: Though the brokers must work inside the boundaries given by the administrative specialists, they do have the circumspection to make minor revisions in the laid necessities called "house prerequisites." A broker-vendor may order a client as a pattern day trader by bringing them under their more extensive meaning of a pattern day trader. Additionally, brokerage firms may force higher-margin prerequisites or confine buying power. Therefore, there can be varieties relying on the broker-seller you decide to trade with.

Day trading on margin is a very unsafe exercise and ought not to be attempted by fledglings. Individuals who have involvement with day trading additionally should be cautious when utilizing the margin for the equivalent. Using margin gives traders an improved buying power, be that as it may, it ought to be used wisely for day trading with the goal that traders don't wind up bringing about colossal losses. Confining yourself to limits set for the margin record can diminish the margin calls and thus the necessity for extra assets if you are attempting day trading just because, don't explore different avenues regarding a margin account.

Market Risk

Market risk is the chance of a speculator encountering losses because of components that influence the general execution of the budgetary markets wherein the individual in question is included. Market risk, additionally called "deliberate risk," can't be killed through broadening. However, it very well may be supported against in different manners. Wellsprings of market risk incorporate downturns, political disturbance, changes in loan costs, cataclysmic events, and fear monger assaults. Methodical or market risk will, in general, impact the whole market simultaneously.

This can diverge from unsystematic risk, which is attractive to a particular organization or industry. Otherwise called "nonsystematic risk," "explicit risk," "diversifiable risk," or "leftover risk," with regards to an investment portfolio, unsystematic risk can be diminished through expansion.

• Market risk, or calculated risk, influences the presentation of the whole market all the while.

• Because it influences the entire market, it is hard to support as enhancement won't help.

• Market risk may include changes to loan costs, trade rates, international occasions, or downturns.

Market Risk - Understanding Market Risk

Market (precise) risk and explicit risk (unsystematic) make up the two significant classes of investment risk. The most well-known kinds of market risks incorporate loan cost risk, value risk, money risk, and ware risk.

Traded on open market organizations in the United States are required by the Securities and Exchange Commission (SEC) to unveil how their profitability and results might be connected to the presentation of the monetary markets. This necessity is intended to detail an organization's introduction to budgetary risk. For instance, an organization giving subordinate investments or remote trade futures might be more presented to money related risk than organizations that don't give these sorts of investments. This data enables financial specialists and traders to settle on choices dependent on their risk management rules.

Rather than market risk, explicit risk or "unsystematic risk" is tied legitimately to the exhibition of specific security and can be ensured against through investment enhancement. One case of unsystematic risk is an organization going into chapter 11, consequently making it is stock useless to speculators.

Fundamental Types of Market Risk

Financing cost risk covers the volatility that may go with loan fee variances because of essential elements, for example, national bank declarations identified with changes in money related arrangement. This risk is generally pertinent to investments in fixed-pay protections, for example, bonds.

Value risk is the risk engaged with the changing prices of stock investments, and product risk covers the changing prices of wares, for example, raw petroleum and corn.

Money risk, or swapping scale risk, emerges from the adjustment in the price of one cash corresponding to another; financial specialists or firms holding resources in another nation are dependent upon cash risk.

Volatility and Hedging Market Risk

Market risk exists as a result of price changes. The standard deviation of changes in the prices of stocks, monetary forms, or products is alluded to as price volatility. Volatility is appraised in annualized terms and might be communicated as a flat out the number, for example, $10, or a level of the underlying worth, for example, 10%.

Financial specialists can use supporting systems to ensure against volatility and market risk. Focusing on explicit protections, speculators can buy put options to secure against a drawback move, and financial specialists who need to fence an enormous arrangement of stocks can use index options.

Estimating Market Risk

To gauge the market risk, financial specialists and investigators utilize the worth at-risk (VaR) technique. VaR demonstrating is a measurable risk management technique that evaluates a stock or portfolio's likely loss just as the likelihood of that potential loss is happening.

While notable and generally used, the VaR strategy requires certain suspicions that limit its exactness. For instance, it accepts that the cosmetics and substance of the portfolio being estimated are unaltered over a predefined period. Even though this might be adequate for short-term skylines, it might give less precise estimations to long-term investments.

Beta is another crucial risk metric, as it quantifies the volatility or market risk of a security or portfolio in contrast with the market in general; it is utilized in the capital resource estimating model (CAPM) to ascertain the average return of an advantage.